D1575743

WHEN I WAS A BOY
NERUDA CALLED ME POLICARPO

When I Was a Boy Neruda Called Me Policarpo

A MEMOIR BY
POLI DÉLANO

WITH POEMS BY
PABLO NERUDA

TRANSLATED BY
SEAN HIGGINS

PICTURES BY
Manuel Monroy

GROUNDWOOD BOOKS
HOUSE OF ANANSI PRESS
TORON

ACKNOWLEDGMENTS

Groundwood Books is grateful to Agencia Literaria Carmen Balcells, S. A. and the Neruda Foundation for their permission to reprint the following poems by Pablo Neruda.

Reprinted by permission of Farrar, Straus and Giroux, LLC :

"The great tablecloth," from *Extravagaria* by Pablo Neruda, translated by Alastair Reid. Translation copyright © 1974 by Alastair Reid.

"Poetry," from *Isla Negra* by Pablo Neruda, translated by Alastair Reid. Translation copyright © 1981 by Alastair Reid.

Reprinted by permission of City Lights Books from *The Essential Neruda: Selected Poems*, Ed. Mark Eisner:

"I can write the saddest verses," from *Veinte poemas de amor y una canción desesperada* by Pablo Neruda, and "The Heights of Macchu Picchu: XI. Down through the blurred splendor," from *Canto general* by Pablo Neruda, translation copyright © 2004 by Mark Eisner.

"The United Fruit Co.," and "El Fugitivo: XII. To everyone, to you," from *Canto general*, translation copyright © 2004 by Jack Hirschman.

Photo of Pablo Neruda courtesy of Sara Facio

Groundwood Books / House of Anansi Press
110 Spadina Avenue, Suite 801, Toronto, ON M5V 2K4

Distributed in the USA by Publishers Group West
1700 Fourth Street, Berkeley, CA 94710

Library and Archives Canada Cataloguing in Publication
Délano, Poli
When I was a boy Neruda called me Policarpo / by Poli Délano;
translated by Sean Higgins; illustrated by Manuel Monroy.
Translation of: Policarpo y el tío Pablo.
ISBN-13: 978-0-88899-726-5
ISBN-10: 0-88899-726-4
1. Neruda, Pablo, 1904–1973–Juvenile literature. 2. Délano, Poli–Childhood and youth–Juvenile literature. 3. Poets, Chilean–20th century–Biography–Juvenile literature. 4. Authors, Chilean–20th century–Biography–Juvenile literature.
I. Higgins, Sean. II. Monroy, Manuel. III. Title.
PS8098.14.E4Z47 2006   j861'.62   C2005-906990-2

Printed and bound in China

CONTENTS

PROLOGUE

In 1936, the year I was born, my parents were living in Madrid, where they had become close friends with the poet Pablo Neruda, who was also the Chilean consul.

During the early months of that year, as my mother's belly grew, the grownups would talk about me whenever they met at parties or poetry readings.

Would I be a boy or a girl? What would they name me?

Neruda said that I would surely be a boy, and he suggested they name me Policarpo. And that's what they started to call me, even before I was born.

But when I finally came into the world on April 22nd, my mother had second thoughts. Policarpo was too outlandish a name, she thought — one that would make me curse her and all my ancestors when I got older.

So they registered me as Enrique Délano Falcón. But among themselves they continued to call me Policarpo, or Poli, for the rest of my life. And now that I'm a writer that's the name I use in all my books.

After I was born, Pablo Neruda and his wife Delia del Carril moved to Mexico, where my family and I lived with them for a while. My childhood memories are filled with the things that happened during those days — my adventures with Tío Pablo.

The Belligerent Badger

WHEN I was eight years old, my parents and I lived with Tío Pablo and Tía Delia at the Quinta Rosa María, a big old estate outside Mexico City. They said it had once belonged to a famous poet because of the words someone had written in letters the size of wine glasses on one of the dining-room walls.

My loyal heart lies down in the shade.

I didn't understand what the words meant, but I thought they were beautiful.

My Tío Pablo was a poet, too, and maybe that's why he was also given to doing some odd things. One Sunday morning at the big open-air Lagunilla Market, he bought an embalmed kangaroo and a skull small enough to have belonged to a dead child. He also had a collection of sea shells of all shapes and sizes, gathered from all the oceans of the world.

The yard at Quinta Rosa María was terribly overgrown, so you could not really tell where the yard ended and the woods began. It was full of weeds and wild underbrush — so different from any other gardens I knew.

On the other hand, it was much better for games and adventures. I could traipse through the wilds of La Quinta like Tarzan, hunting birds and trapping lizards.

The pool in the garden was always empty, very dirty, and full of leaves and branches that fell from the walnut, jacaranda and avocado trees around it. It was as if the grownups didn't even care about swimming.

The cook's son, Sebastián, and I would go down the ladder to explore the deep end like a couple of boy scouts. Sebastián knew exactly where to find scorpions and tarantulas.

That was also where we often saw the badger.

The giant badger had been given to Tío Pablo for his birthday, and the animal wandered the grounds as free as a cat. In the afternoons, as dusk fell, he liked to come into the house, where he would pace around the dining room or relax, draped against a pillow.

"How's my little Niño?" Tía Delia would say, blowing him kisses. That was his name. Tío Pablo had actually named him El Niño at a real baptism ceremony, complete with guests.

My Tía Delia was fairly eccentric, too, though not as much as Tío Pablo. One morning she came to breakfast wearing one white shoe and one brown one.

"Delia, have you lost your mind?" Tío Pablo said, staring at her feet.

"But, Pablo," my Tía replied. "My other pair of shoes is exactly the same."

It made me laugh so much, I had to excuse myself and go out to the patio.

"How's my little Niño?" I said to the badger. I kneeled down, and I think I even saw him smile.

I never got too close, though, because when he pulled back his snout and bared his fangs, it made my hair stand on end and my knees shake. It reminded me of something my mother had read to me one night. Instead of a nice poem about a mother's love, or a story by the Brothers Grimm, she had been reading the dictionary to answer a question I had asked. And she came across this entry:

Badger. A carnivorous animal.

I was old enough to know what carnivorous meant. And I wondered, how could they let this savage creature just wander all over the house? El Niño seemed friendly enough, and some guests even tried to give him treats or pat him, but I knew enough to be wary.

Once, a lady painter brought a female badger to the house, hoping the two of them would get romantic so a few little badgers might be born. El Niño went crazy over his new friend. He raced around the room, jumping over the furniture, spinning Tío Pablo's globes like tops and running back and forth like a cyclone, dragging the female badger around until he finally strangled her with her own chain.

As the lady painter threw herself onto the sofa and wept, her head in her arms, my Tío insisted that El Niño had killed the female badger by accident.

"Was it an accident?" I asked my mother that night.

"Yes, Policarpo," she said. "Animals don't kill among themselves."

Then I remembered a movie I'd seen, where a lioness grabbed a gazelle by the neck and dragged it into her den to be devoured with her family.

But I didn't say a word.

For some reason, after a few months, we left La Quinta Rosa. My parents and I moved into a light-filled apartment in the city. Best of all, it was only a block away from Chapultepec Park — an enormous park filled with tall trees.

A short time later, Tío Pablo, Tía Delia and El Niño moved into the city, too, right around the corner from our apartment. So I saw them practically every day after all.

They arrived just before Christmas. I was especially happy because we were planning to go to Acapulco for New Year's. I couldn't wait to see the Tarzans — divers who leapt into the sea from the top of a cliff.

My parents and I walked to Tío Pablo's apartment on the morning of Christmas Eve to welcome them to the neighborhood. We took presents, and Tío Pablo's gift made him break into the special smile he wore when he really liked something. It was an antique, a small machine used to apply metal tips to shoelaces. The other present, a crystal ashtray in the shape of a heart, was for Tía Delia.

Tía Delia was still sleeping, so I slipped into her room by myself to wish her a Merry Christmas, and to look at the old maps that covered the walls of the room.

As I went to give her a kiss on the cheek, El Niño came flying out from under the covers and sank his sharp fangs into my left leg, right under my knee.

I fell to the floor screaming in fear and pain. I felt as though my heart was trying to escape from my body.

My parents came running, and then Tío Pablo rushed in, his face covered in shaving cream.

"What's going on?" he yelled.

The grownups tried to beat the badger off my leg — many of their kicks hitting me instead — and finally managed to separate the beast from my bloody, shredded leg.

Today I'm grateful that they saved me from the wild animal, but that Christmas was anything but merry. Instead of opening presents under the tree and listening to "Silent Night," I was in a clinic being stuck with one needle after another. The doctors stitched up my wounds and bandaged my leg, and my parents sat with me until I fell asleep.

When I woke up the next morning, my first

thought was that we would not be going to Acapulco as my parents had promised.

I would not be seeing the incredible Tarzans. Not this year.

Before the next summer, my Tía and Tío moved to a bigger house in the Zona Rosa. Their old apartment wasn't large enough to hold all the things they collected every Sunday at the Lagunilla Market. Music boxes, old instruments that no longer worked, African masks, little ships in bottles, marble figurines and bells.

My mother told me that in their new house El Niño attacked their maid, a sweet woman named Virginia, and nearly killed her. They found him biting her neck while blood streamed out.

Tía Delia helped her up, laid her down on the sofa and wrapped an alcohol-dipped towel around her neck like a scarf.

"Poor dear, you'll be all right," she told her, patting her head. But they had to rush her to the hospital.

Now, Tío Pablo really liked Virginia, because she was always so cheerful and competent, and after that attack he finally realized it was just too dangerous to keep El Niño in the house. So after a long discussion with Tía Delia, they decided to donate the badger to the zoo in Chapultepec Park.

I don't know why, but even I felt sad when I heard the news.

One Saturday morning, months later, Tía Delia

invited me to go with her to visit El Niño. I didn't really want to go, but how could I say no?

We looked in every cage before we finally found him. He was slumped down and stretched out, with his eyes closed and a very bored look on his face.

Tía Delia peered at him sadly through the bars, and I'm sure I even saw her shed two or three tears.

"Niño," she called to him in a trembling voice. "How are they treating you, my Niño?"

The badger opened his eyes, raised his head, yawned and looked right at her. Then he got up and walked over to the bars, holding up his front paws and letting out a pathetic whimper.

But I stayed well back. All I could think was that if El Niño saw me and recognized me, he might get mad all over again. Or he might just feel sad if he remembered all the blows he'd received that Christmas Eve. I didn't feel there was any need to make him feel worse.

The United Fruit Co.

When the trumpet sounded, everything
on earth was prepared
and Jehovah distributed the world
to Coca Cola Inc., Anaconda,
Ford Motors, and other entities:
The Fruit Company Inc.
reserved the juiciest for itself,
the central coast of my land,
the sweet waist of America.
It re-baptized the lands
"Banana Republics"
and on the sleeping dead,
on the restless heroes
who'd conquered greatness,
liberty and flags,
it founded a comic opera:
it alienated free wills,
gave crowns of Caesar as gifts,
unsheathed jealousy, attracted
the dictatorship of the flies,
Trujillo flies, Tachos flies,
Carias flies, Martinez flies,
Ubico flies, flies soppy
with humble blood and marmelade,

drunken flies that buzz
around common graves,
circus flies, learned flies
adept at tyranny.

The Company disembarks
among the bloodthirsty flies,
brim-filling their boats that slide
with the coffee and fruit treasure
of our submerged lands like trays.

Meanwhile, along the sugared-up
abysms of the ports,
indians fall over, buried
in the morning mist:
a body rolls, a thing
without a name, a fallen number,
a bunch of dead fruit
spills into the pile of rot.

TRANSLATED BY JACK HIRSCHMAN

The War

My father had hung a poster on our dining-room wall. It was one of Tío Pablo's poems, and it included words like "the time and the water," and "the heavens and the apple."

I understood almost nothing about what the poem meant, but I read it to myself every afternoon, and I liked the way it sounded.

One morning I stopped in front of the poster and began to read the verses out loud, imitating the way Tío Pablo would read. My mother stood there with her mouth open, and when I had finished she ran to call my Tía and Tío on the phone to tell them about my astounding feat.

The poem was about a city called Stalingrad.

I knew the word Stalingrad, because my father took me to the cinema every Saturday afternoon, and Stalingrad came up pretty often in the news-reels they showed before the films. Stalingrad was at war — a war where there was a great deal of snow. It was a Russian city that the German air force was bombing.

In one newsreel, two little girls who were crossing a street disappeared when a bomb fell right in the middle of the road. I cried when I saw those two girls being killed, because for some reason I really liked one of them.

I also really liked the movie that followed the newsreel. I liked it as much as a Tarzan movie I'd once seen in the same theater, where Tarzan battles a giant spider who wants to eat Boy, the son of Tarzan and Jane.

Tío Pablo loved the fact that I'd read his poem out loud, and my mother said he told all his friends about it. He even sent me a letter written in his trademark green ink, telling me I would soon "own the light."

And a few days later he sent me a package. In it were two huge cardboard boats with little cannons that shot tiny wooden rockets.

"So your father can play," Tío Pablo told me when he came to visit.

I stared at him, wondering why, then, he had given the present to me. He explained that it took two people to play with the boats, because one person had to be the enemy, and since I didn't have any brothers or sisters…

The truth is, I hardy ever played with those boats. I didn't like war games.

The war seemed to be very important. Wherever you went, that's all people talked about.

"Extra! Extra!" the newsboys shouted from every

corner. In the newsreels at the movies, tanks roamed through the desert with barrels poking out from their turrets like elephants with their trunks held high. German dive bombers flew almost at roof level to bomb entire cities. Men jumped out of planes with their white parachutes opening in mid-air.

Everywhere there were dead bodies blown all over the fields and city streets, just like those poor little Russian girls lying in the snow.

At dinner, my parents would catch up on the latest news and talk about who had won or lost which battle. If the Germans had lost, they were happy.

And whenever the children in my building got together, we always played war games. If the rain kept us indoors, we played with our toy soldiers. When we gathered in Chapultepec Park, we would divide into two sides to play Army.

It made me nervous, but you had to play.

One night I dreamed I was at the beach — a beach just like the one at Acapulco. All of a sudden Hitler came right up to the rock where I was sitting. He had a short thick moustache and an odd patch of skin on his forehead, and he was wearing big baggy pants, leather boots and carrying a riding crop.

Before I could yell out or even speak, he jabbed a big needle right into my neck.

I woke up startled, sweating buckets, and I must have cried out because my mother was right there, a bit frightened herself.

I told her about my dream and she started to laugh, which made me angry.

After that dream, I added Hitler's name to a list I kept at the back of my handwriting notebook, along with Frankenstein, Dracula and the Wolfman.

"It was just a nightmare, Policarpín," my mother told me, stroking my hair. "Fortunately, Hitler is very far away and he can't hurt you."

That must have been true, because here in Mexico City there were no bombs falling, and when I went down to the street and looked up, all I could see were the volcanoes — Popá and Itza. No paratroopers jumping from airplanes.

The war may have been far away, but I worried that it might somehow draw near just the same.

Almost every weekend we would go some place new with my Tía and Tío. On Sunday mornings we would look through the weird junk at the Lagunilla Market, and my father and Tío Pablo would argue about which of them would get a beautiful antique ship's wheel that they both wanted. Sometimes we headed out on a Friday afternoon and didn't get back until Sunday night. We went swimming in these filthy, stinking pools near Cuautla, where I would wade and swim like a fish with my inflatable lifesaver. Sometimes we visited the beautiful churches in a town called Cholul, high on a hill. We even went as far as Querétaro, so my mother and Tía Delia could buy some translucent stones to be made into rings.

Once, after a trip to the grottos of Cacahuamilpa, we passed through Cuernavaca to get a bite to eat.

The restaurant was in a large, roofed patio with arches in its white walls and a garden full of banana trees and big, thick canes of bamboo. There were so many flowers that just being there made me happy.

My parents, Tío Pablo and Tía Delia and two other friends drank some beer to start off. They ordered a lemonade for me. Soon after that, they asked the waiter to bring dishes of rabbit and bottles of red wine.

A soft wind swayed the branches of the trees. It felt lovely just to be there, even though there were no other children to play with.

At another table there was a group of blond men and women who laughed loudly and talked like they had sore throats. But when the grownups at our table began to sing, the other group began to say things and make gestures with their hands. I couldn't really see what was going on because all of a sudden, my father took me by the hand and pushed me under the table, telling me not to move.

At the cinema I had seen movies with cowboys and Indians. They didn't fight battles with tanks or airplanes but with arrows and rifles. The horsemen fell from their horses the way flies fall when you spray them with insecticide. There were also brawls in town in a room full of tables where some cowboys sat playing cards, and a long bar where others stood drinking liquor out of glasses so small they almost made me laugh.

In those old movies some lone stranger would always come in from the street with a revolver on each hip. The swinging doors would squeak in the sudden silence, and everyone would run for cover.

Inevitably, one of the guys at the bar would set down his little glass and turn to face the intruder. He'd ask if maybe the guy was looking for someone, and the intruder would say yes and send him flying with a roundhouse punch in the face. Tables were left in splinters, bottles rolled around the floor, and women in long dresses ran to hide behind curtains.

Then everybody was fighting everyone else, but you didn't know why. Bodies went flying from one side of the room to the other, chandeliers fell from the ceiling, and it seemed like all-out war.

I saw something very similar from my hiding place in that restaurant in Cuernavaca. The folks at our table replied to the Germans, and then the Germans yelled something back.

Then Tía Delia called out, "They're nothing but a bunch of Nazis!" and all the men got up and started fighting just like in the movies — smashing chairs on each other's heads, throwing roundhouse punches left and right, breaking glasses everywhere.

Even my mother and Tía Delia jumped into the fray with the women from the other table, trading slaps and screaming insults. Our friend Gonzalo tried to avoid getting involved, but my father and Tío Pablo were going at it like Hollywood cowboys.

The fight ended abruptly when one of the German guys smashed Tío Pablo on the head with something that must have been really hard, because it split his head open, and we had to rush him to the hospital.

Of course, the Germans disappeared. Tío Pablo had blood running down his face, and his whole shirt was stained red.

It was all so shocking, I didn't know what to say.

I thought maybe the war had finally arrived right here in Mexico, and now I could tell my friends at home that I had got to see it up close.

Twenty Love Poems:
20. I can write the saddest verses

I can write the saddest verses tonight.

Write, for example "The night is shattered with stars,
    twinkling blue, in the distance."

The night wind spins in the sky and sings.

I can write the saddest verses tonight.
I loved her, and sometimes she loved me too.

On nights like this I held her in my arms.
I kissed her so many times beneath the infinite sky.

She loved me, at times I loved her too.
How not to have loved her great still eyes.

I can write the saddest verses tonight.
To think that I don't have her. To feel that I have lost her.

To hear the immense night, more immense without her.
And the verse falls onto my soul like dew onto grass.

What difference that my love could not keep her.
The night is shattered, full of stars, and she is not with me.

That's all. In the distance someone sings. In the distance.
My soul is not at peace with having lost her.

As if to bring her closer, my gaze searches for her.
My heart searches for her, and she is not with me.

The same night that whitens the same trees.
We, of then, now are no longer the same.

I no longer love her, it's true, but how much I loved her.
My voice searched for the wind that would touch her ear.

Another's. She will be another's. As before my kisses.
Her voice, her bright body. Her infinite eyes.

I no longer love her, it's true, but maybe I love her.
Love is so short, and forgetting is so long.

Because on nights like this I held her in my arms,
my soul is not at peace with having lost her.

Though this may be the final sorrow she causes me,
and these the last verses I write for her.

TRANSLATED BY MARK EISNER

The Spoiled Spider

W E WERE spending our vacation in a big house with colorful gardens, tall trees with thick trunks, and tons of birds. Not just the kind that fly free in the sky or from bush to bush, but the ones that live with the family. We had two huge parrots. They weren't green like most parrots. They were red with blue, yellow and purple feathers and were called macaws.

At the end of the garden there was a low rock wall where you could sit and look out on a narrow cobblestone road that ran down the hill to the town of San Miguel de Allende. You could see the small streets winding between the houses and the tall tower where the church bells chimed in the afternoon. It all looked very pretty, and it made me want to go down there.

It was July. School was out and I had two books my mother had given me for my ninth birthday — *Chinese Fairy Tales* and another one without pictures, *The Kids on Paul Street*.

But I read very little that summer, because my Tío Pablo had a new project — looking for bugs under rocks and fallen tree trunks. And my father had given me a butterfly net.

My parents and Tía Delia slept in almost every day, because they stayed up late playing cards with the owners of the house. But Tío Pablo spent the mornings sitting on the patio writing on some blank pages that he had torn out of a notebook. He wrote his poems in the same green ink he used to write letters.

Sometimes I would go to his table to show him an insect that I'd caught in one of the glass jars I took along on my expeditions.

"That's a yellow wood sorrel," he would tell me, or, "It looks like a scorpion, but it's missing its tail and its stinger. Besides, it only has six legs."

One day, the owner of the house (whom I called Tío Fernando, although he wasn't really my Tío) said he was going to cook some meat in a hole he had dug in the ground. He called it a barbecue.

At noon, we were all on the patio, when suddenly Tío Fernando, who had gone to look for some tongs, returned smiling broadly and waving a green branch in his hand.

"It's huge!" my Tío Pablo said happily, getting up from his chair.

That's when I noticed that the branch moved.

"How fantastic. It *is* a monster!" my father said. "I have never seen such a big walking stick!"

We gathered excitedly around Tío Fernando and I almost couldn't believe my eyes — a small thick branch with thinner branches growing out of it, all moving, and two large round eyes.

"That's a walking stick?" I asked. "Does it bite?"

"Yes, an insect. They say it bites and that it can even kill a horse with its venom. But it's not true. It feeds on leaves and doesn't need to kill anyone."

"Why don't we throw him in with Renata?" asked Tía Lupe, Tío Fernando's wife.

"Who's Renata?" I asked, thinking they were about to torture some poor girl.

"A tarantula this big," Tía Lupe said, curling her fingers up like a spider. "I caught it the other afternoon."

"And her name is Renata?"

"Well, when you have an animal in the house, you have to give it a name, don't you think, Policarpo?" She tousled my hair with her tarantula hand, and it gave me the chills.

"Yes," said Tío Fernando. "Let's throw them in together and see what happens."

My Tía walked to the house and a little while later came back with a square wooden box that she placed on the table where we were going to eat. She opened it slowly. Then she put her hand inside and when she pulled it out, she was holding Renata — wriggling, enormous and hairy.

It was horrible.

"Throw him in," she said.

Tío Fernando put his hand in the box and released the walking stick. Then she threw in the tarantula and closed the lid.

"Something has to happen," my father said. "I vote for the walking stick."

"My money is on the spider," my mother said.

At that moment Tío Pablo looked at me and smiled, raising his eyebrows. And I knew he was asking me whether I remembered the Spider Woman.

Did I remember, Tío Pablo? Did I remember the summer we went to a fair in a little town beside a wide, deep river that ran into the ocean near Veracruz?

Nothing had ever impressed me so much.

And as the adults made their bets, it all came back to me like a movie.

At the fair there were merry-go-rounds, magicians who could pull dozens of silk handkerchiefs from their mouths, noisy puppets that fought and slapped each other, rifles to knock down a moving row of metal ducks.

And, at a special tent lit by two lanterns, a big colorful sign with the picture of a very sad woman said, *Come in and learn the story of the Spider Woman.*

Tío Pablo paid for our tickets. Then he took my hand.

I could see nothing inside the tent, but whispers echoed all around.

Suddenly, from a kind of hole below us, a light came on and the woman from the sign appeared, looking at us as if she was begging for help.

Then a stronger light came on, and I almost ran out of the tent.

Because the woman was not a woman at all, but a gigantic spider with a woman's head and enormous feet that moved. She was inside a box down in that hole, full of live yellow and orange tarantulas that quivered like bubbles in boiling water.

Tío Pablo must have felt me shaking, because he squeezed my hand, while I wondered how many spiders were down there and how there could possibly be a tarantula woman.

Then she told us her story.

"When I was a girl, I lived in a small city as radiant as Paradise," she said. "It was a place full of flowers and lakes with clear shimmering waters, where lovely black-necked swans lived along with the most beautiful birds. Evil was not known there. The word sin did not exist."

The Spider Woman spoke as if she were choking, almost as if she were crying.

"Nevertheless," she continued, "an unknown force entered my soul when I was sleeping one night — a force that drew me down the wrong path. I began to lie and annoy my parents just for the pleasure of it. I stole from my siblings, my neighbors. That's how I grew up, a girl very different from the others in that small kingdom.

"Then the time came for me to marry. Eulogio was an idiot, but marriage was the custom. I began to think of ways to humiliate him. One day, just as I was trying to decide how I could make him my slave forever, a luminous floating being appeared in my room and stared harshly at me.

"'I am Eulogio's guardian angel, and I am here to protect him. If you harm him, if you cause him any permanent damage, you will be severely punished for the rest of your life.' Then the angel disappeared.

"I decided that the greatest humiliation for Eulogio would be for me to fail to show up at our wedding. This would not cause him any permanent damage, and I would not be severely punished.

"So instead of going to the church dressed in my white bridal gown, I walked through the forest toward a lake of emerald waters. As I walked, I happily imagined the scene that would soon play out inside the church. I took a deep breath. The world was mine, and I was the queen.

"Suddenly I realized with horror that I was no longer walking on two legs, but on these eight horrible feet."

The woman burst into tears then, and she sobbed until she could speak no more.

"What a story, right?" Tío Pablo said as we walked out of the tent. I wanted to ask him if he thought it was true, but I could not get the words out.

For several nights after that, I had trouble sleeping because the sad face of the Spider Woman frightened me so, but it also broke my heart.

How could Tío Pablo think I would ever forget her?

The meat that Tío Fernando cooked on the barbecue that night was delicious, and while the grownups happily made their tacos and drank their beers, I continued to look for bugs under rocks.

But every so often, I would creep into the house

and slide over to the table where the box with the tarantula and the walking stick sat. I didn't dare open it, but I pressed my ear against the side of the box and listened...

When it started to get late, the crickets began to sing, and the maids began to clear the plates from the table.

Tía Lupe stood up.

"I think it's time to see who won the bet," she said.

I followed her into the house and came back out with her. I wouldn't have missed that moment for anything.

She placed the box in the middle of the table.

"Ladies and gentlemen, my dear audience," she announced, sounding just like a circus ringmaster. "This is a great, exciting moment. We will now know if this great battle was won by the portentous walking stick that my husband Fernando caught today, or by Renata the pampered tarantula."

We were all on our feet, staring at the box. My Tía began to open it slowly...

Inside, Renata paced nervously. All that remained of the walking stick was the piece of a foot, like a poor branch that the spider ignored.

Some adults won the bet. Others lost. But I am almost certain that Tía Lupe knew very well what was going to happen.

Would she ever have put her precious spider at risk?

I don't think so.

The Heights of Macchu Picchu: XI. Down through the blurred splendor

Down through the blurred splendor,
down through the night of stone, let me plunge my hand
and let the ancient heart of the forgotten
throb within me
like a bird imprisoned for a thousand years!
Today let me forget this joy which is wider than the sea,
because man is wider than the sea and all her islands,
and one must fall into him as into a well in order to rise from
        the depths
with a branch of secret water and sunken truths.
Let me forget, wide stone, the powerful proportion,
the transcendent measurement, the honeycombed stones,
and from the square today let me slide
my hand along the hypotenuse of haircloth and bitter blood.
When the furious condor, like a horseshoe of red-cased
        wings,
hammers my temples in the order of flight
and the hurricane of carnivorous feathers sweeps the
        shadowed dust
of the slanting stairways, I don't see the swift beast,
I don't see the blind cycle of its claws,

I see the ancient being, a servant, the one asleep
in the fields, I see a body, a thousand bodies, one man, one
    thousand women,
below the black gust, blackened by rain and night,
with the heavy stone of the statue:
Juan Stonecutter, son of Wiracocha,
Juan Coldeater, son of the green star,
Juan Barefooted, grandson of the turquoise,
rise up and be born with me, brother.

TRANSLATED BY MARK EISNER

The Tarzans of Acapulco

FTER the morning Tío Pablo's badger chomped on my leg and almost left me lame, a whole year went by before my dream of spending a Christmas on the Acapulco beaches came true.

We had traveled almost a whole day when my Tía and Tío's car broke down in a place that looked like the deserts you see in cowboy movies. I looked in all directions in case I ran into the Lone Ranger or Roy Rogers on his horse Trigger.

It happened very close to a city, quite ugly, named Chilpancingo, where we had to go to find a mechanic's shop. On the way, we ran over a really thick snake that was crossing the road, because the car jumped slightly forward and then back a bit. At least that's what Gabriel, Tío Pablo's chauffeur, said — that we'd gone over a big snake.

By Christmas Eve we were all comfortably settled in the Hotel La Quebrada in Acapulco. I couldn't wait to see the famous Tarzans. My classmate Pirra was always talking about how you could watch them dive into the sea from the top of a huge cliff.

Not only that, but the next evening would be Christmas.

It had taken all day to drive to Acapulco, and by the time we got there I was so tired that when my mother told me to lie down and that she'd bring a sandwich and a glass of milk to my room later, I didn't even complain. I fell asleep before "dinner" arrived, dreaming about the ocean, the beaches and the Tarzans.

I wanted to learn how to dive, too, but only from the lowest diving board at the pool. I still remembered the time Pirra had landed on his stomach instead of head first, and he said his skin had burned all night.

My problem was that I didn't even know how to swim.

That night, I had a nice dream. My father was fishing from a rock. My mother and Tía Delia were eating cotton candy and looking for sea shells, conches and sea stars on a very long, sandy beach. Tío Pablo was strolling in his red-and-blue striped bathing suit and asking us all to watch what he was about to do.

But before he could do it, my father's fishing rod bent just like an archery bow, and he began to reel in whatever it was he had caught.

"I've got something!" he shouted, until a small, two-headed shark emerged. It was biting one of the hooks, flapping its tail. A small octopus with long arms was also tangled in the line.

"Look what I caught!" my father yelled at the top

of his lungs. "A bicephalous shark and a long-armed octopus!"

How odd, I thought. Just a few days earlier I had learned in school that bicephalous meant two-headed, and a little girl had called me Long Arms when I pulled her braids during recess.

It seems that anything can happen in dreams, right? Like seeing Tío Pablo in a bathing suit. Tío Pablo who never went in the water, not even a swimming pool.

After breakfast on Christmas morning, we went down to the beach. My father spent the day fishing from a rock, just like in my dream. Of course, Tío Pablo did not put on a bathing suit. He never wore one, although in his apartment on the desk where he wrote, there was a picture of him — looking much younger and thinner — underneath a coconut tree, wearing a bathing suit with a top like the ones women used to wear.

Instead, now, he rolled up his pants and walked barefoot with his pipe in his mouth. Tía Delia and my mother gathered sea shells, just like in my dream.

When I was about to go in the water, my mother came running with an inflatable life preserver. I put it on.

Three things happened that morning. The first was that my father caught a fish. Not a bicephalous shark or a long-armed octopus, of course, but he did pull out a brilliant blue fish that shone in the sunlight.

The second thing was that Tío Pablo walked

over to a mound of rocks and began to shout, "We have to get her. Get her, Policarpo! We can bake her for dinner!"

A reddish iguana was running across the sand. It was about the same size as the ones we ate some Sundays at the Salto de San Anton, near Cuernavaca.

The third and most important thing that happened was that I learned to swim.

With my life preserver around my waist, I was playing in some small waves. Whenever there were no large waves coming in, I would wander farther into the deep water, just like the bolder kids.

After playing for a while, I turned around and swam to shore, but when I was almost there, I noticed that all the air had come out of my life preserver. So I kept swimming as if nothing had happened.

The second time I went in the water, I told my parents, Tía and Tío to watch, and I showed them how I swam between the waves.

That night I was dying to see my gifts, but my mother sent me to bed early, saying that the sun, the sea salt and tropical heat had exhausted me. She told me that when I woke up, there would be presents at the foot of my bed.

At first I tried not to sleep and wondered what my gifts would be, but I did not even last two minutes before my eyes closed.

I rubbed my eyes so they would open wide and I could take in all my gifts. As soon as I saw the packages on the dresser, I jumped out of bed and began to take off the colored paper.

A pair of sandals. Not fair, I thought. I just wanted toys.

Then, a machine gun that shot out small flames!

Next, no. Two T-shirts. A blue one with white stripes and a red one with yellow stripes.

But then, yes! A box with lead soldiers, some on horseback.

Ugh. Three pairs of socks.

The last package was small and soft. I tore off the paper and found a pair of foam glasses, very ugly, that looked like the ones aviators wore in the movies. On a card, written in green ink, was a picture of an anchor and the words, "So you can learn to swim under water. Your Tío Pablo."

The things my Tío did!

Later that morning we went to a beach that was more than an hour away, where the water was supposed to be like on a postcard — calm, and almost transparent blue — and the sand was so fine, almost white.

"The water here is so pure and calm," Tío Pablo said when we were settled on beach chairs in the shade of a palapa, "that you can clearly see all the fauna."

"What is fauna?" I asked.

"The sea animals," he said. "Marine fauna. Fishes, octopuses, clams, snails, seahorses and narwhal..."

Seahorses and narwhal! The things my Tío said!

"Enrique," he called out to my father. "We could go and order some live clams, don't you think?"

My father thought it was a good idea.

"What are seahorses and narwhals?" I asked.

"I like that you are curious, Policarpo. Seahorses are those precious horses from the ocean that swim standing up and roll in their tails. The narwhal is the immense and fearless marine unicorn."

I didn't believe a word of it.

"I gave you the glasses so you can admire that fauna and get to know the flora. Put them on and go out and duck under the water!"

"Flora? You mean Flora Mendoza from my school?"

"Fauna are the animals. Flora are the vegetables — the algae, the seaweed."

I tried to remember everything he told me. My Tío Pablo knew a lot. He must have written some poems about flora and fauna.

I put on the glasses and the life preserver, although I already knew how to swim. Then I took a deep breath and into the water I dove!

It was like going into another world. When I put my head underwater I found a blue fish like the one my father had caught. I saw yellow fishes with black stripes, fish that blew up like balloons, and those standing seahorses.

I put my hand out but was never able to reach them. Maybe the glasses were magnified and the fauna was farther away than it seemed.

"I like your gift very much," I told Tío Pablo later.

That afternoon, when it began to get dark, we all settled at a table in the hotel with a view of the high quebrada — the cliff where several Tarzans were going to jump head first into the ocean.

I had only seen dives like that before when we went to a place called the Salto de San Anton, where men jumped into the water and people gave them money.

In Acapulco, the quebrada was much higher. The ocean roared in and out between the cliffs in rough, angry waves.

I was the only one who went over to the jump-off point to watch the divers fall head first into the water that lay below like a big round pool. My parents, Tía and Tío preferred to sit in the restaurant and drink coconut milk with some kind of liquor before they ordered the iguana platters.

The first Tarzan arrived at his spot and a hush came over the people in the dining room. From below, someone gave a signal and the guy jumped up. Then, opening his arms like the wings of a plane, he turned in the air and landed head first in the water. Later he came up swimming and climbed up the rocks to the hotel veranda, where he received a lot of applause and lots of bills.

"I want to be a diver when I grow up," I said.

"It can be a great career," Tío Pablo said, looking cheerfully at my mother. "You'll have to start practising right now."

But my mother was not smiling. She shook her head as if to say, "That Pablo!"

"I'll start tomorrow," I said.

The Fugitive:
XII. To everyone, to you

To everyone, to you,
silent beings of the night
who took my hand in the darkness, to you,
lamps,
of immortal light, star lines,
bread of the living, secret brothers,
to everyone, to you,
I say: there's no thanks,
nothing could fill the cups
of purity,
nothing can
contain all of the sun in the flags
of the invincible springtime
like your quiet dignities.
Only
I'm thinking
maybe I've been worthy of so much
simplicity, of a flower so pure,
maybe I'm you, that's right,
that essence, flower and song of earth,
that natural kneading that knows
where it comes from and where it belongs.
I'm no distant bell

nor a crystal buried so deep
you can't figure it out, I'm just
the people, hidden door, dark bread
and when you receive me you receive yourself
in your very self, in that guest
beaten so many times
and so many times
reborn.

     To all and everyone
to all I don't know, who'll never
hear this name, to those who live
along our long rivers,
at the foot of volcanoes, in the sulphuric
copper shadow, to fishermen and peasants,
to blue indians on the shore
of lakes sparkling like glass,
to the shoemaker who at this moment questions,
nailing leather with ancient hands,
to you, to whomever without knowing it has waited for me,
I belong and recognize and sing.

TRANSLATED BY JACK HIRSCHMAN

Caviar for Tía Ant

I WAS doing my math homework and my father was listening to his favorite tango program on the radio when the phone rang. My mother answered. I perked up my ears and realized it was Tía Delia. In other words, the conversation was going to last a while.

From time to time I managed to catch phrases like "I'm worried that he might be a nuisance and make things more difficult for you both," (surely the nuisance was me) or, "Sunday without fail, because I don't like him to miss classes," and, "Well, I'll talk to him and call you back."

My mother hung up and leaned against the doorway.

"Would you like to go to Oaxaca for a few days?" she asked me. "With Tío Pablo and Tía Hormiguita?" Her nickname was Hormiguita, which means Ant.

"To Oaxaca?" I said, opening my eyes wide. One of my classmates had been there for vacation and he said there were some very old ruins nearby. He also said there was a tree so big that it took forty people joining hands to reach around it, and every afternoon in the plaza there was live marimba music.

"Yes!" I shouted, very excited. "Yes, Mother, I want to go!"

Although there would be no other children, I always had a great time with Tío Pablo, and I wasn't the least bit worried about going by myself.

So on the Thursday morning of Holy Week, we set out in Tío Pablo's car driven by Gabriel, his kind chauffeur.

Around three o'clock in the afternoon we passed through a town by a lagoon where fishermen would catch little fish that they fried and sold in packages like popcorn or potato chips, dry and crunchy.

"This is the place where they cook monkey, right, Gabriel? The little monkeys are very delicious."

Tío Pablo had pretty strange tastes, including a fondness for exotic dishes. Friends would send him bear meat, fish eggs, Chinese snakes and Japanese insects from all over the world. It was really unbelievable. On Sundays we would take all-day trips to Cuernavaca to eat iguana in a restaurant near Salto de San Antón.

"It's good enough to make you lick your whiskers," my Tío would say. My father liked it, too, but my mother and Tía Delia always ordered chicken or beef instead. Before the main course my father and Tío would drink beer or coconut milk and eat tiny quail eggs with chopped onion and hot sauce.

One Sunday we passed the market and saw my Tío eating worms that were being cooked right there in a frying pan. They were maguey worms, and the truth is that I found it disgusting, but only a little.

Then there was the time my parents, some friends and I drove my Tío to a painter's house in Tepoztlán, where he was planning to write a long poem. He was going to stay there for about a week so he could "work quietly," he said.

When we arrived, the owner of the house, who had about fifty little Pekinese dogs, served us juice made from the Jamaica flower and invited me to go for a swim in the pool. After I had dried off and got dressed, we all said goodbye to Tío Pablo.

"Are you driving straight back to the city?" he asked as he walked us out to the station wagon.

"No," said my father. "First we're going to a hacienda near Cuernavaca. It's famous for its goat roasted on coals."

My Tío thought for a moment.

"Goat roasted on coals?" he whispered. After several minutes, as we finished packing everything into the car, he said, "Wait a minute. I'm going to get my suitcase."

So instead of staying to write his poem, he left with us for the Hacienda de Cocoyoc. Just to eat roasted goat.

Still, it seemed depressing to stop at every little wooden food hut just to see if they prepared monkey.

How could you eat a monkey? Wasn't it almost the same as eating a person, no matter how delicious it might be?

Fortunately, we had bad, or rather good, luck. None of the restaurants in town served monkey, which had to be ordered several days in advance, first because they had to hunt it, and second because it took a long time to prepare.

Tío Pablo put on a disappointed face.

"Should we order it for your return visit, Don Pablo?" asked Gabriel.

"No, Gabriel. If they had it ready, I would have liked to try it. But to order someone to hunt a monkey is something else. It's almost like asking someone to kill a child."

As we left that town and continued on to Oaxaca, Gabriel changed channels on the radio until he found a song that he liked.

"The Bandit," he said.

"Which bandit?" Tía Ant asked in alarm.

"Graciela Olmos, the woman who composed this song — they call her Bandit," Gabriel explained.

"What lovely lyrics," said Tío Pablo. The song said that the horizons would be singing in Irapuato.

"The Mexican people can create such poetry," said my Tío. "Don't you think it's fantastic, a song about singing horizons? It's fabulous, the notion of horizons singing in the dusk. Can you imagine? A polyphonic chorus of horizons…"

"No, no, Don Pablo," said Gabriel. "What it means is that there is a musical group named the Horizons, and they are singing in Irapuato."

My Tío remained quiet for several minutes and then said, "The Mexicans certainly have a sense of humor." And he began to laugh.

My Tía laughed, too. They laughed for several miles.

We pulled into Oaxaca that night, and the hotel was right on the plaza. I went straight to the balcony and opened the window so I could listen to the marimba players, but they must have finished playing for the day, because they were nowhere to be found.

In the morning, we went to the market right after breakfast. My Tía and Tío had already been there on another trip to Oaxaca and they wanted to buy some green pottery mermaids that they said were unique to the area. They bought four mermaids (one for my parents) as well as some plates, cups and other things for the table, all in the same green pattern.

But the strangest thing my Tío did that morning was to buy a bag of grasshoppers. They were no different from the grasshoppers that we used to hunt on the patio and in the country. My Tía Ant told him that he was disgusting when she saw him put lime and spicy powder on them and then stuff several into his mouth.

"You don't know what you're missing," he said. "They are delicious."

He offered me the bag and I was quite prepared to tell him no, thank you, but for some reason the exact opposite happened, and I took one.

To be honest the bugs didn't seem that bad to me. At least they were cooked and not alive, like the bugs I once saw a little girl eating in the plaza in Cuautla. They looked like black beetles. One escaped from her mouth and walked across her cheek.

"Ay, Pablo, how can you eat that?" my Tía said with a look of disgust.

"It is good to try everything," he replied. "Remember what Diego told us, that he had eaten human flesh, and that the tastiest bit is the meaty part of the hand."

Diego was a fat man with eyes like a toad. He painted very large paintings and from time to time he and a very attractive woman in a wheelchair would visit my Tía and Tío when we lived in Quinta Rosa María.

"Well, that's all right. Human flesh, yes, but not insects."

I couldn't believe my ears. Had she was it was all right to eat human flesh?

"Insects, no! Frogs, sea cucumbers, deer, wild boar — anything — but not insects!" insisted my Tía.

"All right, all right," said my Tío, laughing. "No insects. Tonight I will order Champagne in the hotel and we will have it with some caviar that was sent to me from Denmark."

My Tía flashed him a sweet smile.

As I've said, she was somewhat eccentric, too. My mother told me she had been born in Argentina and that her family was so rich that once when she was a child and they were traveling by ship to Europe, her parents bought a ticket for a cow so she and her brothers could enjoy fresh milk during the trip.

That night, the marimba players arrived right after dark. Tío Pablo decided that my Tía and I should go down to the plaza to hear them up close, while he prepared the crackers and caviar and sent for the bottle of Champagne that had been chilling.

People were gathered in front of a stand where

three musicians were playing "La Llorona," a song my father loved. It was about the ghost of a crying woman who is cursed to roam the earth after she drowns her own children. He especially liked the part that went, "I am like green chili, crying woman. Spicy, but delicious."

My Tía bought me some cotton candy, the kind that leaves you sticky all over. She said she would wait for the caviar. We listened to the music for about half an hour and then went back to the hotel. We had to go to bed early that night, because the next morning we were going to see the famous Tule Tree, the one that was so big that it took forty people to reach around it.

Back in the room, Tío Pablo was waiting for us. He smiled, pointed at a tray of crackers with caviar on the table and began to open the bottle of Champagne a little bit at a time. The cork made a popping sound as it bounced off the ceiling, and foam bubbled out of the bottle as he filled two glasses. There was a soft drink for me.

Then he began to serve the caviar.

"Hmmm, how delicious!" said my Tía as she ate enthusiastically.

Tío Pablo looked over and winked.

I looked at my Tía a little sadly, because I knew that what was on the crackers was not caviar at all but prepared ants that had been sent to my Tío from who knew where. But I had promised him that I would not say a word.

Besides, the ants didn't taste so bad to me.

The Great Tablecloth

When they were called to the table,
the tyrants came rushing
with their temporary ladies,
it was fine to watch the women pass
like wasps with big bosoms
followed by those pale
and unfortunate public tigers.

The peasant in the field ate
his poor quota of bread,
he was alone, it was late,
he was surrounded by wheat,
but he had no more bread,
he ate it with grim teeth,
looking at it with hard eyes.

In the blue hour of eating,
the infinite hour of the roast,
the poet abandons his lyre,
takes up his knife and fork,
puts his glass on the table,
and the fishermen attend
the little sea of the soup bowl.
Burning potatoes protest

among the tongues of oil.
The lamb is gold on its coals
and the onion undresses.
It is sad to eat in dinner clothes,
like eating in a coffin,
but eating in convents
is like eating underground.

Eating alone is a disappointment,
but not eating matters more,
is hollow and green, has thorns
like a chain of fish hooks
trailing from the heart,
clawing at your insides.

Hunger feels like pincers,
like the bite of crabs,
it burns, burns and has no fire.
Hunger is a cold fire.
Let us sit down soon to eat
with all those who haven't eaten;
let us spread great tablecloths,
put salt in the lakes of the world,
set up planetary bakeries,
tables with strawberries in snow,
and a plate like the moon itself
from which we can all eat.

For now I ask no more
than the justice of eating.

TRANSLATED BY ALASTAIR REID

An Invisible Stroke of Fate

O N SUNDAY afternoons my parents would
often get together with Tío Pablo and Tía
Delia to enjoy what they called an aperitif.
I usually said I wanted one, too, so they would serve
me a glass of lemonade or Jamaica flower water.

It was on one of those Sundays that a feeling of
dread suddenly came over me as I listened to them,
because instead of their usual conversation about
Chilean poets or how the war was progressing, they
were talking about taking a trip to New York.

"We have to go, Enrique," Tío Pablo said to my
father. "We have to experience that city, since we are
so close."

"It will be a long trip by car," said Tía Delia.

"Yes, but it will also be very interesting to travel
across northern Mexico."

"But what about the child?" asked my mother.

I knew she was talking about me, Policarpo. The
bad thing was that I couldn't go to New York with
them, because I was not on vacation. And because
we didn't have any relatives in Mexico with whom I

could stay during the month that they would be away, I knew there was only one solution.

Boarding school.

My stomach rose up into my throat at the thought, but at the same time the idea appealed to me. I would always see the boarding students from my school playing and laughing together at recess. They always seemed to be having a good time.

Several days later, my parents left me at the boarding school with a suitcase full of clothes and another smaller suitcase that held my notebooks, a ruler, a compass and a pouch with pencils, erasers and a pencil sharpener.

And although I was nervous, I thought that maybe here, far from my house, I might finally be able to stop crying over what had just happened to my little dog …

Every morning, my father would take my little dachshund, Poroto, to Chapultepec Park. They usually returned to the apartment just as I was finishing my breakfast.

But on that morning he did not come back as usual, and I had to leave for school before he returned.

I was sitting on the curb across from the Chapultepec Cinema, waiting for the car that took me to school every day, when I saw my father walking toward the apartment. He looked very tired, and his eyes were full of tears.

He was alone, and in one hand he held a green leash.

My first morning as a boarding student was the same as all my other mornings. Class and recess, eating gummy worms and apple candies sold from a stand in the school patio.

But the afternoon was different. While we were doing our homework before the snack, several bigger boys gathered around and informed me that because I was the new kid in the boarding school, they would have to "baptize" me. They said every boy had to go through it.

So I was forced to go with them to the dormitory bathroom, where other boys were waiting. And there, in front of all these boys, I had to get in the cold shower fully clothed.

Mother, Father, why didn't you take me with you to New York, I said to myself as I cried inside.

I spent a week in the infirmary with an attack of the asthmatic bronchitis that I sometimes got. When the lady who was taking care of me — a fat, pleasant older woman — said that I was well enough to return to classes, I asked her if maybe it might be best for me to remain there for a few more days.

But she saw right through me.

The next three weeks passed slowly, and then one day it was all over. My parents, my Tía and Tío arrived, all very happy about their trip. Once again I could sleep in my own bed surrounded by the insect farms, shells and other strange things Tío Pablo had given me.

I was also very happy with the gifts they had brought me from New York. A baseball glove, a kit for building bridges and towers and wheels of fortune and — best of all — a large bow and six real arrows with metal tips and blue feathers.

"That's so you can defend yourself from cowboys and other bad guys," my Tío Pablo winked at me. I didn't know what he was talking about, but I gave him a big thank-you hug anyway.

Several days later I asked Tía Delia what he had meant by other bad guys. She explained that the cowboys attacked the Indians with rifles, and the Indians defended themselves with arrows.

"But I like to be the cowboy," I protested. "And I have a rifle, too."

"The Indians are the good guys, Policarpo," she said firmly.

As I've said, my Tía and Tío were pretty strange.

One Sunday morning, my parents, my Tía and Tío and I went on a picnic in the country to try out my new archery set and glove. We stopped to pick up Pirra, a friend from school who was a little older than me. He was the son of Spanish refugees.

We set everything up near the Pyramids of Teotihuacán. While my mother and Tía Delia spread out the tablecloths and all the things that we were going to eat, my father and Tío Pablo drank a bottle of wine. Pirra and I played baseball. We took turns using the glove.

The day was as happy as we were, with a cloudless sky, and the volcanoes were white with snow. I think we all felt content.

"Damn, I forgot the silverware!" shouted Tía Delia. She was always forgetting something.

After we ate some hard-boiled eggs, sausage sandwiches and cucumber salad with our hands, Tío Pablo suggested that we try out my new bow, and he said that I should shoot the first arrow. There were six of us, one for each arrow, and after we had shot them all (my father's traveled the farthest), Pirra and I set out to gather them up. The sun was already bright and hot.

After a long time we had only found five arrows. There was one missing.

"You go and look in those bushes," Pirra said. "I'll head toward the stream." So we split up.

After much searching I suddenly let out a very loud yell.

"Pirra!" I yelled at the top of my lungs. "Come here! Mother, Tío Pablo, come everyone!"

I couldn't believe what I was seeing. The arrow was embedded in the ground and had passed right through a snake that looked like it was made of caramel, with red and black stripes.

"Incredible!" said my father.

"It looks like an imitation coral snake," said Tío Pablo very calmly, after he had examined it.

"What do you mean, imitation?" my father exclaimed angrily. "Can't you see it's a real snake?"

"Yes, it's a real snake, but it's an imitation coral snake. The coral snake is a viper and this one isn't."

"Oh, Pablito, what are you talking about?" said my mother. "And what's the difference? Snake, viper, serpent — they're all the same."

Tío Pablo looked at them with his little smile.

"The difference, of course, little girls, is the venom. Vipers, which are poisonous, have triangular heads, while snakes, which are not, have oval-shaped heads."

I believed everything Tío Pablo said, because he knew a lot about nature. He wrote about it in his poems.

I looked at the viper — I mean, snake — and I realized he was right. It looked just like the coral snake, only its head was the shape of an oval.

After the initial shock wore off, I knew I wasn't prepared to lose an arrow. It had to come out. I was wondering how I felt about that when, as luck would have it, Pirra grabbed the end of the arrow, put his foot on the snake and pulled the arrow until it came loose.

"Unbelievable," said Tío Pablo, shaking his head. "It is…fate."

"Fate? What do you mean, fate?" Pirra and I didn't really understand what the word meant. Tía Delia wanted to explain it to us.

"If you are walking down the street and you stop to tie your shoelaces, and one step in front of you a flowerpot falls from a window, then fate has favored you. If, however, you do not stop and the flowerpot falls right on your head, then fate has treated you poorly."

My Tío and father looked at her as if to say that her explanation was far too complicated, but I understood it just fine. Fate was what had happened to my dog, Poroto.

I took one last look at the snake. It was a victim of fate, too. The ants were already gathering around the round hole that the arrow had left in its body.

"Those ants don't waste any time," said Tío Pablo, as he glanced teasingly at my Tía Ant.

We set off for home. Luckily not the boarding school.

Poetry

And it was at that age...poetry arrived
in search of me. I don't know, I don't know where
it came from, from winter or a river.
I don't know how or when,
no, they weren't voices, they were not
words, nor silence,
but from a street it called me,
from the branches of the night,
abruptly from the others,
among raging fires
or returning alone,
there it was, without a face,
and it touched me.

I didn't know what to say, my mouth
had no way
with names,
my eyes were blind,
my soul,
fever or forgotten wings,
and I made my own way,
deciphering
that fire,
and I wrote the first, faint line,

faint, without substance, pure
nonsense,
pure wisdom
of one who knows nothing,
and suddenly I saw
the heavens
unfastened
and open,
planets,
palpitating plantations,
the darkness perforated,
riddled
with arrows, fire and flowers,
the overpowering night, the universe.

And I, tiny being,
drunk with the great starry
void,
likeness, image of
mystery,
felt myself a pure part
of the abyss,
I wheeled with the stars.
My heart broke loose with the wind.

TRANSLATED BY ALASTAIR REID

Like Taking a Bone from a Dog

WHEN we moved from the Quinta Rosa María country house to the apartment on Paseo de la Reforma, I learned what it meant to lose something. I had lost that backyard forest with its mysterious nooks, the trips to the bottom of the pool to search for tarantulas and scorpions, the alligator and chameleon hunts, and those thick, tall trees full of branches that my friend Sebastián and I would climb in the afternoons when we got home from school.

Living in an apartment was something else entirely. But luckily our new street had tree-lined gardens down the center, and Chapultepec Park was very close by. The zoo where they took El Niño, my Tío Pablo's badger, was located there. There was also a lake where my father and I would sometimes go very early in the morning. We would rent a small boat and, while my father rowed, I would throw breadcrumbs into the water from the back of the boat, prompting a line of swans to follow us.

Once my Tío Pablo came rowing with us. He and Tía Delia rented another boat and we drifted off, calling out to one another from one boat to the other, although it was difficult, because my Tío's boat tended to lag behind. Even though my Tía loved the swans, they never wanted to go again because Tío Pablo had got blisters on his hands from using the oars.

In the afternoons, after I had done my homework while my father listened to his tangos on the radio, I would go out to play with Rene, Gustavo and other boys from the building, or I would go for a walk by myself. Sometimes I went all the way to Pirra's house to play with him and his sister, Mercedes.

One night, while Tío Pablo and Tía Delia were visiting, I went into the living room and told the four adults that I needed a job because I wanted to buy myself a Sheaffer fountain pen and an Omega watch.

Tía Ant started to laugh.

"And can you tell us why you need a fountain pen and a watch?" she asked.

"Yes," I replied. "The fountain pen is to write with, and the watch is to tell time."

Then my Tío started to laugh.

"But this boy is exceptional," she went on. "Did you hear that answer?"

"If you want to work," my father said, "on Saturday you can shine all my shoes. For pay, of course."

"Of course," I said.

"Work is the means of support that will enable one and all to enjoy abundance," my Tío said, though I didn't understand him. Maybe it was from one of his poems.

One afternoon after it stopped raining, I left the building and headed to the movie theater. The Chapultepec Cinema was right across from the Diana, a round fountain with a statue of a naked huntress about to release an arrow from her bow. The cinema had just opened the week before with a Walt Disney movie.

I looked at the posters for the movies they were showing and noticed some children my age who were selling boxes of Adams chewing gum to the people going inside. I remembered the commercial from the radio: "Daddy, buy me some chewing gum. Adams chewing gum." The boy who said the words was younger than I was, but he had such an irritating voice that I just wanted to kill him.

The little boxes of gum were yellow, green and pink, depending on the flavor.

That was when I had a great idea.

The next day, I took the money that my father had paid me for shining his seven pairs of shoes, plus a few pesos that I got from my mother for helping her with some chores around the house. At the kiosk at school, I bought about forty small boxes of Adams gum.

In the afternoon, after homework and the tangos, I arranged the gum in my pencil box and headed back to the cinema.

I'd already sold more than ten boxes and was feeling pretty happy when the other chewing gum boys came over. They looked kind of angry.

"Hey, you," said one. "Why don't you take off? There's no room for three of us here!"

I didn't know what to say. I was a little afraid they were going to beat me up.

"But why me?"

"Because we were here first, you stupid idiot." They started giving me little shoves toward the sidewalk and when we reached the edge, they pushed me even harder. Then they kicked my butt and yelled at me, telling me that if they saw me around again, they would bash my head in.

Those were their very words. "Bash your head in."

I started walking back to my building, close to tears. Why could they sell gum and I couldn't?

I went into the apartment and locked myself in my room. When my heartbeat finally slowed down, I counted the rest of the gum boxes and the coins I had received.

I had definitely done well. I already had a little more money than I had spent, and I still had half the gum left.

But what was I going to do now?

A few days later, still thinking about the fountain pen and the Omega watch, I decided to go into a new business. I put on some fairly old gray overalls that were a bit too small, got two kitchen towels from my mother and headed back to the cinema. On my way there I looked up at Diana and crossed my fingers.

The people who drove to the cinema would park their cars along the side street next to Paseo de la

Reforma, and I had already seen other boys do what I was planning to do.

A gray-haired man got out of his car after parking it on the street. I walked over to him.

"Are you going to the movies?" I asked.

"Yes, child."

"Would you like me to take care of your car?"

"All right, but take good care of it. Or are you the kind that doesn't do a good job?"

Not only was I planning to take care of his car, I was also going to polish it using one of my towels. The tip would be good.

That afternoon I managed to get three customers, and I returned home with four twenty-peso coins and a fifty-peso coin. The only bad thing was that since the show was two hours long, I had to stay there until all the customers came back out.

When I arrived home later than usual and quite dirty, I got a pretty good scolding.

Tía Ant, who was there without Tío Pablo, defended me.

"He is a splendid child," she told my mother. "Don't scold him. You have to let him grow up."

The next day, Saturday, a little before seven in the evening, I went back to my business.

I was still trying to get a customer when a boy a bit taller than me approached.

"Get lost!" he yelled. "We don't want you around here!"

Again, as with the chewing gum incident, I didn't know what to say. I stood there like a fool, not moving and just wondering why he could stay and I had to leave. Wasn't there enough room for everyone?

My body felt cold and my knees trembled.

"Did you hear me, kid? Get lost, unless you want me to kick you out!"

"But…"

That's when I felt the punch in the nose. I fell to the ground. I must have hit my head because I saw stars. Really, I saw stars and I don't mean the ones up in the sky.

When I got up, my nose was swollen and bloody.

"Do you want some more?" the bully asked me.

"No," I said, and headed home with my tail between my legs, just like a dog. I felt as though there was no room for me in this world.

Before I went up to our apartment on the third floor, I dried my tears and cleaned the blood off my face and neck. Tío Pablo would probably be there, and I didn't want him or my parents asking me any questions.

I opened the door very carefully, closed it without a sound and tiptoed to my room.

Just as I put my hand on the doorknob, my mother's voice hit me like a pail of icy water.

"Policarpo!"

I stopped.

"Yes?"

"Come and say hello."

I ran my hands over my eyes once again and went back to the living room.

"Hi, Tío Pablo. Hi, Tía Delia," I said.

But I didn't manage to fool anyone. They asked me what had happened. At first I said nothing, but I gave up. My parents, Pablo and Tía all knew me too well.

"It's just that…I…I had a problem…"

"A problem?" asked my mother. "What problem? Were you in a fight?"

"Let's see. Come here," called my father. I went over and he examined my bruised nose and burning eyes.

"It looks like you've been bleeding, Policarpo," Tío Pablo said, very serious.

"Poor boy. We have to treat those wounds. He's in pretty bad shape," said Tía Delia.

"But first he's going to tell us everything that happened," said my mother. "And when I say everything, I mean everything."

So I had no choice but to tell them about my whole adventure, from the chewing gum business all the way up to the punch I had just received. That damned Chapultepec Cinema, I thought. The things it had got me into. I told myself I would never go back.

But then I remembered Diana, and I imagined myself climbing up the statue, taking her bow and shooting poison arrows at the boys who had treated me so badly.

In the bathroom, my mother washed my face with warm water and that felt good and soft, even though it hurt. Then she put ointment under my eyes and around my nose. Finally she filled a little bag with ice to reduce the swelling.

We went back to the living room, where Tío Pablo was enthusiastically praising an old map that my father had bought cheaply at the Lagunilla Market.

"Hurray for the hero of the day!" he said in a loud voice when he saw me.

A hero? Me? My Tío was teasing again, as usual.

"When a dog has a bone in his muzzle," he said, looking at me seriously, "it's very difficult to take it away from him. He'll defend it to the end."

I didn't know what he was talking about. My Tío often spoke in riddles.

"Have you seen any gangster movies?" he asked.

"Yes," I answered excitedly. "I saw Angels with Dirty Faces." And I started to tell him about it.

"I saw it, too," he interrupted. "But if you pay attention, you'll see that the gangsters only shoot to defend their own territory — what in war is called the zone of influence. Just like dogs do when they have a bone."

"Why are you telling me all this, Tío?" I complained. He was starting to make me angry.

"Because you have become an invader, Policarpo," he answered.

"An invader? Me?"

"Those boys who sell chewing gum and the boy who takes care of cars — they were already there when you arrived."

"But I wasn't bothering them."

"Of course you were. Quite a bit, as a matter of fact. If someone buys gum from you, then he won't buy it from one of them. Do you understand? That's called competition. If this had happened among gangsters, they would have killed you without a second thought. When you have something, you don't let go of it easily. You tried to take the bone from the dog and the dog didn't let you."

I began to understand.

"Besides, my Niño," said my Tía, who had taken to calling me Niño after her old badger. "You were selling gum to buy yourself a fountain pen and a watch, right? But those other children do it to buy food for their families."

Things were becoming much clearer.

One afternoon my mother took me to see a Tarzan movie at the cinema. While she was buying the tickets, I noticed one of the boys who was out selling gum. He looked at me, and I'm not sure whether he recognized me or not, but I suddenly wondered whether he had ever gone into the theater with his mother to see a movie.

And at that moment, things finally became absolutely clear. And I understood.

BIOGRAPHICAL NOTE

Photo: Sara Facio

PABLO NERUDA was one of those rare people — a genius. What Wolfgang Amadeus Mozart was to music, what Leonardo da Vinci was to painting, Neruda was to poetry. King Midas could touch anything and turn it into gold. Neruda's strength lay in his use of language. Words, images and rhythms were the tools he used to transform human lives, emotions, and the most ordinary everyday things into the most marvelous poetic expression. With words, images and rhythm, Neruda turned everything into poetry.

He was born on July 12, 1904, in the small town of Parral, in central Chile. His original name was Neftalí Reyes Basoalto, but he changed it to Pablo Neruda when he turned sixteen because he already knew that he was destined to write, and Neftalí did not seem to be a proper name for a poet.

Sadly, his mother, Rosa Basoalto, had passed away just a few months after he was born. Two years later his father, José del Carmen, a railway engineer, remarried and moved his family to the nearby city of Temuco in Araucanía, a region of southern Chile that was inhabited by the indigenous Mapuche people long before the Spanish conquistadors arrived. There the young boy grew up surrounded by a landscape of great trees and greenness in what is probably one of the rainiest places on earth. And there he developed his powerful curiosity about nature, something that would always have a kind of intoxicating effect on him. At the age of ten it already made him feel like a poet, even though he did not yet write poetry. As Neruda himself recounted about his childhood, "I was attracted by birds, beetles and partridge eggs... I was amazed by the perfection of insects." He also developed a love of books, which became his companions during his solitary days in the south. He read so much — Emilio Salgari, Jules Verne, Victor Hugo — that at times he even forgot to eat and sleep.

When Neruda was fourteen, his first poems were published in a local magazine. At about that same time, a new principal arrived at his school. He described her as "tall, with very long dresses and flat shoes, dressed in the color of sand." She was Gabriela Mistral, the great Chilean poet who would receive the Nobel Prize in Literature in 1945.

After he finished school, Neruda decided to move to Santiago, attend university and become a French teacher. He left the security of his family behind and embarked on a vital and independent period filled with poetic creativity, relationships with writers and Bohemia, friendships and love affairs that soon made him drop his studies so that he could dedicate himself entirely to living and writing. He led a poor existence in various boarding houses in modest neighborhoods and at nineteen dazzled Chilean society with *Twilight*, his first published book. The following year saw the publication of *Twenty Love Poems and a Song of Despair*. It is his best-known book and has been translated into many, many languages.

> I can write the saddest verses tonight.
>
> Write, for example "The night is shattered with stars, twinkling blue, in the distance."

Many men have confessed to attempting to win over their girlfriends by uttering beautiful lines like these, pretending that they were their own.

In 1927, as a result of the prestige Neruda had earned with his new, intense, profound poetry that seemed to delight one and all, the Chilean government brought him into the Foreign Service and sent him as consul to Rangoon in Burma. He spent about five years in various Asian countries, serving as consul in Rangoon, Colombo, and Singapore among other faraway places. He experienced a terrible loneliness. In his memoirs, he recounted how in one country he felt the need to teach his servant Spanish so he could read him the poems he was writing.

Far from the provincial city of Santiago, Neruda had leapt into the world, where despite his loneliness he became impassioned by people, places and native artefacts, whether conches, masks, jade statues, ancient books or paintings. He started to amass his fabulous collections of art, handicrafts and antiques, which still fill his homes — now museums — in Isla Negra, Valparaiso and Santiago.

It was during these solitary Asian days, after a turbulent love affair with a young and very jealous Burmese woman (whom he named Josie Bliss and introduced in his poem, "The Widower's Tango"), that he married a Dutch woman, Maria Antonieta Hagenaar, with whom he had a daughter, Malva Marina, who was always very sickly, finally dying at the age of eight.

Though he returned to Chile, Neruda's wanderlust led him to travel to Argentina (1933), where he became a great friend of the famous, doomed Spanish poet Federico García Lorca. It was in Barcelona (1934) and Madrid (1935), during the bloody civil war that shook Spain, that he acquired new notions about the condition and fate of the world. Lorca's murder by fascist forces, and the growth of German Nazism and Italian Fascism intensified his interest in progressive politics and gave his poetry a greater clarity, which he expressed in his incendiary book, *Spain in My Heart*. It was also at this time that he met and fell in love with the Argentine painter Delia del Carril, also known as "Hormiguita" (Little Ant).

Between 1940 and 1943, Neruda and Delia lived in Mexico, another country that had a powerful influence on him due to its history, colors, art, cuisine and people. There he was part of a very powerful literary and artistic circle that included Diego Rivera and Frida Kahlo. On his way back to Chile, he stopped in several countries along the Pacific coast of South America. In Peru, he scaled Macchu Picchu, the greatness of which inspired one of his most beautiful poems.

In 1945 Neruda received Chile's National Literary Award, and that same year he was elected senator of the Communist Party, which he had recently joined. In 1948, as the Cold War began to take hold in the world, the Chilean government of González Videla began a campaign of repression against miners and others seeking their rights as workers. Neruda became actively involved in a very bitter strike and gave a famous speech, "I accuse" where he read out the names of striking miners who had been imprisoned by the government. As a result, he was stripped of his post as senator and a warrant was put out for his arrest.

The poet and his wife were forced into hiding from the authorities for many months, as they moved from one friend's house to the next. His friends not only risked their lives by hiding him, they had to put up with his many possessions, his need for good food, and his intense desire to continue to see many people especially at dinner parties where drinking and conversation went on into the wee hours, making it very difficult to keep his presence a secret. During those days, he worked feverishly on what would turn out to be one of his greatest works, "General Song."

At the beginning of 1949 Neruda made a spectacular and very dangerous escape aided by some friends and a couple of mountain mule drivers. He managed to flee the country by crossing the Andes Mountains in the snow on horseback. As he was a very large man and had not ridden a horse in decades, it was extraordinary that he was able to reach the Republic of Argentina, which he entered bearing a fake passport that identified him as an ornithologist named Antonio Ruiz. He spent the next three years in exile traveling through Europe, the Soviet Union, China and the countries of the Eastern Bloc. In 1952, he was free to return to Chile, for which he had felt great nostalgia, as he expressed in his poem written while in exile, "When from Chile."

In the fifties, sixties and seventies, Neruda's fame grew immensely. He became a rich man, very rare for a poet, because his books were so popular all over the world. He loved to meet and recite his poetry to people who were poor, marginal and dispossessed. They reciprocated his affection. He also knew and befriended writers all over the world and, as always, was irresistibly drawn to many women. The poet had turned fifty when he married Matilde Urrutia, who was his companion until his death and to whom he dedicated his beautiful poem, "The Captain's Verses," as well as *One Hundred Love Sonnets*.

Neruda continued to be a strong progressive voice and worked actively to elect Salvador Allende president of Chile. Allende was the first elected socialist in the Americas and in 1970, he named Neruda Chilean ambassador to Paris. In 1971 Neruda was awarded the Nobel Prize in Literature but shortly after he discovered that he was suffering from advanced cancer. He returned to his beloved Santiago where he died on September 23, 1973, only twelve days after Allende was killed and the elected government was overthrown by Augusto Pinochet, inaugurating a severe military dictatorship. His funeral turned into a massive political protest, a shout of rebellion against dictatorship.